Curious George®

Trash into T

Adaptation by Bethany V. Freitas

**Based on the TV series teleplay
written by Bill Burnett**

Houghton Mifflin Harcourt
Boston   New York

For information about permission to reproduce selections from this book, write to trade.permissions@hmhco.com or to Permissions, Houghton Mifflin Harcourt Publishing Company, 3 Park Avenue, 19th Floor, New York, New York 10016.

ISBN: 978-1-328-57745-0 paper over board
ISBN: 978-1-328-57746-7 paperback

Cover art adaptation by Artful Doodlers Ltd.

hmhco.com
curiousgeorge.com

Printed in China
SCP 10 9 8 7 6 5 4 3 2 1
4500745917

AGES	GRADES	GUIDED READING LEVEL	READING RECOVERY LEVEL	LEXILE ® LEVEL
5-7	1	J	17	530L

George was excited for Pretty City Day!

Everyone wanted to pick up trash and
make the city pretty. But George's team
wanted to win, too.

"Teams will be judged on how much trash they collect, how pretty their streets are, and their can-do spirit!" said the mayor. "Good luck!"

Each person on George's team had a street
to clean. George's street was already pretty
pretty.

But look!
A candy wrapper!
George put it in his trash bag.

George was so busy
looking at his pretty
street that he didn't see the
pile of boxes until it was too late. *Crash!*

8

His neighbor heard the noise. "Take anything you want," he said. "Just put the rest back in the boxes."

At least now George had some trash to pick up! But why would anyone throw out a pirate ship?

George wanted to keep it. He had an idea: he would use one of his bags for trash and one of his bags for treasure.

The longer George
walked, the more
treasure he found.

George's treasure bag got heavy fast. He needed to empty it, so he went home.

He had found so many great things.
A red bottle. A blue clock. A few yellow ducks.

George had always loved the man's pig
collection. Now he had a collection of
his own! A street treasure collection.

Meanwhile, the mayor was outside, weighing the team's trash. "We need George's bags, too, if we're going to win," Steve said. "Where is he?"

Upstairs, the man and Steve couldn't believe their eyes! "George, why is your trash all over the floor?" But this wasn't trash! It was George's collection.

"George, a collection is a group of things
that are alike. Find some things that go
together and make that your collection.
Then bring the rest to the mayor, okay?"

George looked at his treasure. There were round things and things made of wood. Red things and things that could float. George wanted to keep them all!

When George finally brought his bag to
the mayor, it was still empty.
"There might be more trash upstairs," the
man said. "Let's all go check."

And there was. But it sure didn't look like trash anymore. "A color collection? Way to go, George!" said Steve. Even the mayor was impressed.

They may not have collected the most trash
but what better way to celebrate Pretty City
Day than to turn trash into something
beautiful?

Collect Them All!

George saw that lots of his treasures went together in different ways. There were round things and things made of wood. Red things and things that could float. George wanted to keep them all! Look at the images below and see how they go together in different ways. How can you sort them? What kinds of collections could you make?

Recycled Bird Feeder

You can keep trash out of the landfill and make some neat things with recycled materials, just like George. Want to make your outside space extra pretty? Next time you finish a roll of toilet paper, use it to make a bird feeder!

You'll need:

- **Empty toilet paper tube**
- **Butter knife**
- **Paper plate**
- **Nut butter or sunflower butter**
- **Birdseed**
- **Ribbon or string**

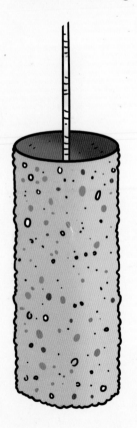

What to do:

1. **Use the knife to spread a thin layer of butter all over the outside of your toilet paper tube.**

2. **Pour birdseed onto the plate. Roll your buttered tube in the seed, carefully pressing to coat.**

3. **Thread ribbon or string through the hole in the tube and knot the ends to form a loop.**

4. **Hang your bird feeder from a tree branch and wait to see what feathered neighbors stop by for a snack. Now, isn't that pretty?**